# EMBRACING

## —THE—

# SEASONS

# EMBRACING
## — THE —
# SEASONS

*Memories of a Country Garden*

GUNILLA NORRIS

BlueBridge

Parts of this book were first published as *Journeying in Place*.

Published by
B l u e B r i d g e
An imprint of
United Tribes Media Inc.
Katonah, New York

www.bluebridgebooks.com

ISBN: 9781629190051

Library of Congress Control Number: 2015904218

*Cover design by Cynthia Dunne*
*Cover image: Richard Felber / Photodisc / Getty Images*
*Text design by Cynthia Dunne*

Printed in the United States of America

10  9  8  7  6  5  4  3  2  1

# Contents

# FALL

# WINTER

# SPRING AGAIN

## AT THE CENTER

*The alders tremble*
*at the edge of the field.*
*A green enthusiasm.*
*Each year they come*
*a little closer to the middle.*
*One day they will be at the center.*
*They are like us*
*in this desire to move,*
*to reach out*
*into bud and leaf,*
*to feel who we are*
*in the presence of others.*

# Introduction

This is a soulful journey through a country garden and the surrounding land with its stone walls, its brook, its hemlocks and maples, its flowers and shrubs, and its various living beings. It is a journey through the seasons of a year. Journey is perhaps too active a word, for it implies a distance traveled from here to there. I do not mean that. I mean instead a circling in time, in *one* place, remembering one year as if it were all years.

I no longer live there. But I have been deeply shaped by my time in that country place. The land and all that I perceived in it entered my being while I conducted my so-called ordinary life of eating, sleeping, and earning a living.

I want to go into memory now, to relive my past experiences and to share them. My farming ancestors knew how to embrace all seasons. When the fields were harvested and the soil turned, when the ground was frozen and the trees had lost their leaves, they were freed from their usual labors. Time could be spent in other ways, in storytelling, in fellowship, in preparing and repairing, in planning and reflecting, in remembering. I want to follow in their footsteps.

My home in the country was an old farmhouse that was surrounded by a little more than two acres. Once the farm itself was big. It had pastures, woodlots, fields, orchards, and gardens. When I lived there, a lawn and a stand of ash trees grew where the apple orchard had once flourished. The dead, gnarled trunks remained as evidence. A little pond at the back of the property might have been a drinking place for cattle in the past.

Over time I learned that in these two acres, intense but mostly quiet activity was happening twenty-four hours a day. I missed a lot of it, getting caught up in what had to be done in my daily routine, and therefore failed to truly experience the sunsets, the budding of the raspberries, the rusting of old farm tools in the earth, the building of wasps' nests, the death of old trees. But in some mysterious way I did feel the vibration of it all. In my memory I want to revisit that eventfulness and know it better. Even just a little bit better!

For us to know in this way requires our presence and openness to experience and intimacy. We have to be willing to surrender our goal-setting, direction-oriented, controlling selves, in order to encounter and be encountered, to meet and be met, to know and be known. This is hard for many of us. The urge to be in control is so embedded in our bodies, our education, and our culture that we feel helpless under its sway.

Control and intimacy are mutually exclusive. Intimacy cannot be commanded or planned. It is not willed, but happens by grace and opens the doors of the heart. It more readily happens when we lay no claim to anything and discover instead what is already present and already given.

All true intimacies are gifts. They appear as if from behind us, beside us, above us, below us. We usually cannot see them coming. They take our whole attention, and in the process we have a chance to come face-to-face with something we did not know about the world and ourselves.

To commune, to discover and to be discovered, is deeply human. Real convergences are revelations that lift us out of ourselves, out of recoiling from any aspect of reality. We experience the self then—all possessive pronouns gone—the joy of existence, which is the light within everything, the light that burns for its own sake, declaring, "I am that I am."

The Latin word for "intimate" is *intimus*, "inmost." If we live in an "inmost" manner with our surroundings, we can see and know much more about ourselves and the world. We can experience that each being that dwells with us calls it home, too. To remember, to hold, and to venerate the life around us is to honor the holy in the place where we live. It is also a way to celebrate the earth—the first and primary intimacy from which all other intimacies develop.

I hope as you read that you will think deeply about the place where you live, whether it is in a city, a suburb, a meadow, or a forest. All places contain the sacred. They ask us to participate, to be fully here on earth. The fulcrum of this universe may ultimately be a passionate mutuality in which we surrender any separate definition of ourselves and discover that we are who we are together, in a fundamental relationship and communion with everything that is.

# SPRING

# *Peepers*

These tiny frogs announce the arrival of spring. In the early mornings, their high chorus of trills begins to rise from the pond and the nearby marsh. They are a life sign.

I have never laid eyes on them. But as spring advances, their chorus grows until there is a continuous high pitch day and night. "The waters are warm enough. The sun is warm enough. Live," they sing. "Live!"

I walk along the side of the pond behind the farmhouse. It smells of mud and wet leaves. The peepers stop their singing. My presence must be something strange and perhaps threatening to them. But of course when something feels like that to me I grow quiet, too. There is an ancient animal caution that lies deep inside us, instinctive and necessary. Silence is wedded to the protection of our being. It is only when the caution is continuous and we remain silenced that we are no longer really alive.

As soon as I pass, the peepers take up their song. My heart lifts.

It isn't just the peepers that announce the season. At four in the morning, songbirds are loud in the darkness of dawn. Woodpeckers are drumming, and blackbirds add their calls. They all herald the coming warmth and this burgeoning time of mating and building nests.

Spring is so full of possibility and joy. Why then is there a feeling that the beauty of these weeks is so achingly poignant, and that the soul can hardly hold the gift of it? Is it because all this new life seems so fragile and so perishable to us? Is it because, at some level, we are asked to be more than we think we can be now that winter has gone? Could it be that we can only acknowledge majesty when beauty hurts in such an exquisite way as to penetrate our tough skins? Then we can go beyond our own small sense of the world to be part of the ecstasy of praise.

I hear that ecstasy in the peepers. It is the full voice of *aliveness*, asking us to go beyond our little spheres and to share in the hymn that praises life.

The peepers are singing. Their sound is exuberant. As children we may have been punished for such exuberance. As adults it can be hard then to claim our authentic voices and to use them without shyness. But spring asks us to live with gusto. We are urged to let go of every wintry thought and let it melt away. Pains and struggles of the past are not to be carried into the new season. Perhaps by the sheer dint of these noisy peepers with their fierce insistence we, too, can belt out our songs of praise.

We recognize each other's voices on the phone.
There is a timbre and a quality there.
But there is also another voice that is not
about vocal resonance.
It is about much more.

Our authentic voice, what is it?
Can we learn from the peepers
that praise is that voice—a God-given one,
not ours to possess but ours to pour out?

# Skunk Cabbage

In the low-lying parts of the woodlot, the skunk cabbages poke their hefty leaves out of the mud. They are the free-form sculptures of these woods, and they grow in profusion. You either like them or dislike them. I need to grow to like them, for they have much to teach me.

It is spring in earnest. Mosquito larvae live in the stagnant water between the bright green leaves of the skunk cabbages. Birds call. Buds are knobbing up on the trees and bushes. I feel spring ache in the air. The swollen pregnancy of life pushes forward, bursting at its seams.

Determined to watch the skunk cabbages grow, I have been going out to inspect their progression. The upward surge of the leaves is astounding. You can almost hear them growing, sopping up moisture. They seem to gain an inch a day. This is cabbage intelligence. They must do this while it's wet enough. Perhaps they also do this before the leafy canopy of the trees is shutting out too much of the light for their growth.

Something in me wants to grow, too, when the opportunity presents itself. There is urgency—an "it-won't-wait" feeling. I know I am not alone in having this feeling. But to really experience this, to act on it, is not so easy. It means a special kind of listening and a willingness to open up.

I practice with the cabbages. Are they humming? Buzzing? I sense a vibration without an actual sound. How strange it is that we can somehow hear/feel things of this nature. Can we learn to hear/feel what is in us? Perhaps this is the sound the Bible speaks of: "In the beginning was the Word." Could one meaning be that in the beginning was Vibration? All that exists has been sounded. Are we not configured through this vibration, which is movement and being all at once? We are named by it, oscillated and electromagnetically uttered into life.

To listen, then, to whom and what we are given to be is a profound act of resonance. I think the cabbages do it growing there—squat and flashy—firmly planted in the sump of the woods. They obey their given natures. I want to be as secure in mine, to feel the vibration that is forming me from the soles of my feet to the roots of my hair. A part of that configuring is to bear my drawbacks, the way the cabbages bear their smell. Directly. No psychic deodorant. No cover-up. I want to believe that these stocky green skunks of the woods are giving me, a two-legged friend, hearty encouragement from deep within the muck and ooze of spring and the vernal equinox to be who I really am.

*Hearing inwardly and sensing with the whole body*
*is a way of listening that leads to recognizing*
*and admitting all that we are.*
*We open up.*

*Admitting can mean various things.*
*We admit someone into our home.*
*We recognize something as genuine and true.*
*We own our mistakes and thoughtlessness*
*without cover-up.*

*When we admit our faults and limitations*
*without exaggerating them, excusing them,*
*or using them as leverage for gain,*
*we become more truthful and trustworthy.*
*This can lead to meaningful growth and change.*

# Finches

A pair of finches begins to circle the house in late April. This is their territory. They look for a likely spot and begin gathering twigs, bits of string, pine needles, and other nest-building materials. He is rosy and large. She is mostly grayish brown, and smaller.

The two are now old friends of mine. I like to guess where they'll put their nests. They build two—a false one as a decoy and the real one. The female even sits in the decoy nest to fool the predatory world.

One year the real nest was built in the decorative wreath on the front door. I could not believe my good fortune. I was able to watch their nesting ingenuity from indoors. Unfortunately, someone else was watching, too. Four eggs of a lovely blue-green color were laid. When the eggs were almost ready to hatch, the nest was raided. The neighbor's cat got them all. I was heartbroken.

The finches came back the following year and built a nest on the porch light, a fixture that was higher up than the cat could reach. But from then on I knew that their second, real nest was hidden in a nearby hemlock, while the decoy was easy to spot on that porch light.

We can notice this decoy maneuver in ourselves, too. At times we look very busy about something innocuous to keep safe the brooding and hatching of something precious inside us. We build a decoy activity, so to speak, for we know that too much outside interest directed toward a creative inner process would ruin it. Then nothing can hatch.

To incubate a book, a poem, a drawing, an idea, or a new attitude, we need an inner nest. The twigs of association must be gathered. The materials to make a safe place for incubation must be quietly put together. If this process is disturbed, we have to start over. A whole new nest must be built. But to start over too many times becomes defeating. There is often not enough inspiration and spiritual presence to do that.

Turtles cover their eggs. Finches build decoy nests. Mothers grow silently large with child. We have an instinct to surround the new with time, with protection, with secrecy.

I have yet to see any baby finches. My pair does a good job of protecting their brood. I feel good about their skill in this. New creatures are born for their own sake, for their own lives, not for the benefit of others. I am simply grateful that these two finches find this garden good enough to raise a family in.

*A space is needed between the daytime mind*
*and the creating mind.*
*The daytime mind wants clarity, facts, timeliness,*
*and results.*
*It will do what it thinks is necessary to survive.*

*The creating mind wants space and freedom.*
*It is at home in mystery and in timeless time.*
*More than in stability, it wants to live in the realms*
*of meaning.*

*How do we honor both—since both are necessary?*
*Perhaps we do it by respecting the threshold,*
*the space between them.*
*When we learn not to charge from one state of being*
*to the other,*
*but to transition with care and awareness,*
*we form a habit that honors both.*
*Then something new in us can hatch out*
*with a pair of well-matched and beautiful wings.*

# Dahlias

I go down into the cellar and look for the dahlia tubers from the fall. They are wizened, old-looking things. I can hardly believe these brown and wrinkled lumps of matter are going to be glorious flowers in about two months.

It is May now, and the ground is warming up. Even if we should have one more frost, these tubers will be safe in the ground. I have tried to sort out their colors so that I will have mostly white and yellow flowers. Right now the tubers all look the same, and I have a color roulette on my hands. By July there may be a bank of yellow and white dahlias punctuated by a solitary, flaming red one. A surprise. A red flag. I'll accept that.

I feel glad to be in my shirtsleeves, trowel in hand. Near the west side of the house there is a stone wall. A bed has been dug there, and that is where the dahlias are going.

These are the small variety and do not have to be set very deeply in the ground. I spade up the dirt and put one of the tubers in. By fall, this one will have produced several more, not unlike potatoes. I just have to wait.

This is easy gardening. I like it, and yet I am a little suspicious about easy things. Just pop the tuber in and forget it. If the weather is dry, add water. It's a foolproof recipe. I feel a little ashamed when I get compliments for any of my fast and easy recipes—it seems the results shouldn't be that good with so little effort.

This, of course, is childhood conditioning. Hard is good. Easy is suspicious. These private or cultural evaluations have nothing to do with how things fundamentally are. The intrinsic way may just be the easiest way, and I want to learn to trust that. Standing by the stone wall I ask myself, "What power is doing the growing around here?" And I answer, "Something in the life-force of the dahlias themselves. I am simply present to enjoy their unfolding."

I spade up a place in the bed for each tuber. In they go, and are covered with soil. I do not have to do anything more. I do not have to sweat. The dahlias know what to do. Leaves will come. Flowers will come. Some years they will even be profuse. In the fall, the dahlias will die. I will dig up the tubers. I will put them in the cellar. They will be planted again the following year if all things remain the same. Which is as likely to be true as not to be true.

Can we live this dahlia way, too? It is a way that does not complicate or use force. It is a direct way that allows for process. To be planted, to flower in the sun, and to surrender to frost when it comes is a metaphor for how things occur in every aspect of life. It's living and dying, again and again. This allowing is transparent and profound.

In the gentle May sunshine, with a tuber in each hand, I ask: What is easy? What is hard? I don't know. They are all mixed up in my mind. But I do know that these tubers, these wizened root balls, are full of summer color, full of allowing. As I tuck them into the soil, I want to trust that I am tucked in as well, embedded in that matrix that supports everything. Then whatever color is within me will emerge naturally.

*How quickly we assess and judge things,*
*deciding in a moment's glance if something is worthy*
*or not worthy.*
*Why is a weed not as beautiful and needed as a rose*
*or a dahlia?*
*We divide the world with our judgments—good and bad,*
*easy and difficult.*
*We divide ourselves that way, too,*
*casting important aspects of ourselves into the dustbin.*

*We have the biblical assurance that God created everything*
*and that it was good.*
*We need to trust our inner goodness.*
*We need to take good care of our personal soil.*
*Then we can grow and blossom.*

# Poison Ivy

The poison ivy leaves are beginning to come out on the vines. They are somewhat copper-colored and oily. Poison ivy grows happily around here. In fact, it is the most luxuriant crop on this property. By June its leaves will be glossy and green.

I have learned to respect the plant and watch out for it. A cake of yellow soap is always at hand by the kitchen sink in case I inadvertently brush up against these leaves. Some people handle what is poisonous with poison. They spray, year after year, and eventually some parts of their gardens might be free of the vines.

I do not feel comfortable with this method, for I do not know what other effects I would be causing. But I do not feel comfortable doing nothing, either. Some vines I have just severed, or pulled out of the ground, hoping they would die. But this has very little effect on their profusion.

I notice that wherever there is a great deal of poison ivy, there is also a bounty of jewelweed. From jewelweed an anti-itching salve can be made. Things are often paired like this in nature. They balance each other and form a whole.

This happens in the internal ecology, too. We see in ourselves how an extreme of any kind often creates its opposite. If we fall into work addiction our bodies will sooner or later give out, and we will have to do absolutely nothing for a period of time. If we pride ourselves on being thoughtful and consistently courteous persons, we are sure to turn unexpectedly mean without understanding why.

The poison will form and will find its way to expression. An antidote is needed. This balancing act is also obvious in our food choices. For example, if we eat too much salt we often crave something sweet to counter it, and vice versa.

Poison ivy and jewelweed. Over time it is never just one or the other. How often do we think we are absolutely right about something, and in being adamant we lose the fabric of relatedness and the situation becomes all wrong? We keep forgetting that events arise in relationship to each other. They grow simultaneously. They are neither this nor that—and yet they occur because of this and that. They make each other happen.

Something that looks like poison may lead to something very good. Something seemingly wonderful can have the seeds of destruction in it. We have no way of being sure. Living with such tension is very hard. We will always be right and wrong. Safe and in danger. Strong and weak. Loving and uncaring. Smart and stupid. Aware and unconscious.

I know this as I walk here in the woodlot and despair over the profusion of poisonous leaves. Too much to ever be rid of! These vines are here for good, like the poison ivy aspects inside me. I take comfort in the stately stands of jewelweed that grow here as well, and pray to have jewelweed inside me, too.

With the poison is the jewel. With the jewel is the poison. Ivy and weed, they are my teachers. I hold them in my mind, and a bar of yellow soap in my hand.

*To live honestly in a balanced tension is to be vibrant*
*and alive. But very often we do not know*
*where that balance has its center. Perhaps only in time*
*do the great swings of opposites converge.*
*How many years will it take for the jewelweed to be equal*
*to the poison ivy?*
*How many years will it take for impatience to be balanced*
*by patience or for anger to be balanced with peacefulness?*

*Knowing that there is already an inherent balance,*
*we can better face our imbalances.*

# Quince Tree

The old quince tree is in bloom now. Its little white flowers are such a contrast to its dark brown trunk. They shine and are completely new, while the tree itself looks ancient. Twisted and gnarled, it appears to me like an aged modern dancer whose every limb is going off in some contorted, asymmetrical direction. Here and there bark has peeled off in long strips, to hang like a skimpy dance costume around the exposed trunk.

Every year I think that this will be the last year for the old tree. And then here it is again—in bloom. By late August its furry, pearlike fruit will be hanging there for the birds and for me. Some years there are only two or three quinces. Sometimes I gather as many as ten.

I respect this tree very much. It is the crone of the garden. I would miss its presence greatly should an autumn storm take it down. Its dark shape in the middle of a very green lawn seems appropriate. It is a great-great-grandmother tree that is still bearing fruit. I want to learn from it.

One thing it has taught me is that I can bear fruit even into the later years of my life. It also tells me of the power of roots. This tree would not be standing now without a strong root system holding it in place. I want to believe that I am growing strong roots like that into the ground of my being. And the tree shows me that new flowers are new flowers no matter what the rest looks like, and that beauty comes in many forms.

There are other fruit trees here on the lawn. Two pears.

One peach. Two plums. They are younger trees and they, too, are in bloom just now.

But the long-lived quince tree is different. It is a *presence* that seems to come forward to meet me. I find myself talking to the tree, addressing it with deference. "Old Grandmother," I say, "how are you today?" I swear the tree answers with a groan. Not a complaint. It is an old tree creaking in the wind.

"Nice flowers," I say.

"They'll do," mutters the tree.

"Anything you want?" I continue.

"A little water would be nice. Just leave the hose running and don't fuss. That's the main thing. Don't fuss. Things are just fine the way they are."

"How do I know that they are just fine?"

"You don't until you find it out."

"Please explain, Old Grandmother."

"I will, but only this once. The more you worry, the more worry you have. So don't fuss. Just do or don't do. Second-guessing wastes your life. I'm blooming and that's enough."

I fetch the garden hose. But I don't leave it on by itself. I stand there and water. Just that. I water the old quince tree on this fine day in May.

*Why is it that we think we help things along*
*by fussing over them—rehearsing actions ahead of time*
*or second-guessing after we've acted?*

*Do we feel insignificant if we haven't made waves*
*around our actions?*
*Do we feel too exposed to judgment if we simply act,*
*without worrying excessively about details or results?*
*Or do we feel too free, somehow afraid of the ease*
*and lightness that simply acting—without worry—*
*gives us?*

*Maybe it is only after years of practice that we can*
*blossom—just blossom.*

# Soil

Everything smells so verdant and fresh in the spring. I am drawn outside to grub in the ground. It's the green time, the time to plant the vegetable garden.

Under the leaves of the compost lies new earth. I spade it up bit by bit and heap it up in the wheelbarrow. The soil smells of moisture and nutrients. I am enjoying how black it is—full of organic materials, full of potential.

How to design this year's vegetable garden? One mount for zucchini, one row for sugar peas, one for beans, one each for spinach and chard, one for lettuce. Nooks and crannies for cucumbers that can climb up and over the protective stone wall.

I spread the new earth on last year's rows. Grubbing in the ground feels wonderful. I've become a kid with permission to be dirty. I am getting more than exercise here. Earth-connected, soil-immersed, I am turning everything over.

The rows look handsome now, mounded up and ready. I feel hopeful and expectant. It's preparation time, when all feels possible. Next to the trowel lies an assortment of seed packets and flats of tomatoes, basil, and eggplants. The seeds are all different. Beans, sturdy and singular, can be planted one at a time with precision. The lettuce seeds, on the other hand, are almost poured into place from the packet. A fine, dark dusting is sprinkled down the row to be covered loosely with earth.

Time of planting, depth of planting, proximity of plants to one another—these are all considerations. Eggplant must be moved every year. Tomatoes like the same old place in the garden and flourish well with basil as a companion plant. Snow peas and lettuce like the cool of early summer. Zucchini does well in slightly sandy soil, as do the root crops. It's hard to keep track of all these preferences. But they make the difference between a fine yield and a mediocre one.

Each one of these seed varieties has its own nature, its own way in the garden. If we want a good crop we have to learn about this. Our inner nature, too, has its organic leanings. To go against ourselves will harm our development. We must acknowledge this in us and in others. To really be fruitful we must respect our own nature.

I form lines and poke holes to drop the seeds in. Covered by new soil, each in their own place, the seeds wait for sun, for rain, and for their life force to produce the first delicate showing of green. Each day I will come here to witness it.

Thoroughly dirty from all the grubbing and planting, I sprinkle a little earth on myself for good measure. I, too, am planted in this garden.

*After a dormant or frozen period in life*
*we know we must dig down and turn things up*
*to open us again. Old patterns come to the fore*
*and stagnation is exposed.*

*It may not be the season of spring when we do this.*
*Grubbing for the soul has its own calendar.*
*We might have to prepare our inner ground*
*in a wintry time, or we may have to wait*
*for warmer weather both within ourselves and without.*

*Grubbing is a messy task, but when we are able*
*to understand it as part of our growing,*
*we learn its value and approach it differently.*

# Impatiens

All danger of frost is over now. It is time to plant the impatiens. Parts of the garden are very shady, and these annuals fill in and give color to the place. They like the conditions and do very well here. Their very profusion creates a special richness.

I get many flats of them. For the most part they are the pink variety. Occasionally I buy white ones as well. Into the flowerpots and beds they go. It is rather simple-minded— an all-of-a-kind gardening.

For years I tried other flowers. I wanted variety and flamboyant color. Of course, the most riotous bloomers are plants that need sun. So nothing much came of those experiments in my garden. I had to submit to planting the one annual that does splendidly here—the humble impatiens.

I feel a little exasperation about planting the same flower again this year. But my need for variety is thwarted by very real conditions. Why do I resist the obvious? I plant and try for some equanimity while knowing there's an irony here. I am impatient with these impatiens.

This feeling is a familiar one. We resist repeating the same old thing, whatever it might be, because in the very act of repetition we discover what the real conditions are within us: restlessness, need for reassurance, fear that life is passing us by, the need for distraction and entertainment. We try to find ways around ourselves, resisting the truth.

The circumstances of this garden suit impatiens perfectly.

The circumstances of my life could suit me perfectly, too, if I would allow myself just to be here. I could enjoy this one-of-a-kind gardening and feel its inherent rightness. I could enjoy my life instead of questioning it too much, wondering if I am doing something wrong, or not well enough. I could find satisfaction in simply conducting my work. Life could be without effort. Easy. Why don't I garden and live in this direct way: take up the very same thing again and again, and slowly come to the heart where all things flourish?

I don't have any answers. Resistance and impatience are so familiar. They keep me from surrendering to the obvious, the fluid way of just doing what needs doing, allowing year by year what can grow within me and around me. And that means planting impatiens just now.

*Our habits of impatience and resistance die hard.*
*We think they will get us what we want,*
*even as we know that they separate us from the truth.*

*Perhaps the only way is in the slow, organic growth*
*that happens when we let go and let be,*
*over and over again.*
*Letting go, we enter into the wholeness*
*that already exists and lets us be free.*

# SUMMER

# Peonies

With a bundle of stakes under my arm and a ball of twine in hand I go to the peony bed. It lies in full sun and is crescent-shaped. I stand there and see how leggy the peonies have gotten. Their buds are hard and heavy. Already the plants are bending toward the ground. They need support, and it is time to stake them.

For weeks I have been watching the peonies emerge. At first they are just a hint of red in the dark soil. Then more happens. Something round and headlike pushes upward into the world. It looks bloody, like a birth. Not just one, in fact, but many, many births.

Not long after, solid red stems stand in the crescent bed. Their shapes are visible through the living room window, even in the dark. I always think of them as a tribe of spirit people who have ascended from below, tunneled up from some dream state or territory that once gave them life. Then they are here, eager to live in a new world.

We are born this way, too, emerging into this life from some other place—ready to live where we are planted, ready to be at risk and think nothing of it. At least to begin with.

Now it is June. The peony leaves are growing dark green and glossy. There are fewer leaves on the plants this year, and this gives the illusion that the plants are taller. I place a stake in the middle of a peony clump, cut the twine, and gather the stems in my arms. A peony hug! My hands try to find each other while my face is buried deep in the leaves. I feel my way to making a knot. The circle of twine must close, but not too tightly. With a little tug to make sure that the knot will hold, I let the stems go. They spring back and right themselves. The peonies look braced, and I am aware that they have embraced me, too. In a few days their blossoms will open, and they will be huge.

Human blossoming, too, needs to be staked and supported. We need our family or a circle of friends to hold us if we are going to open and let out the beauty that is in us.

How many of us have keeled over just in the time of blooming for lack of support and encouragement? How many of us have not dared to reveal our true selves because we feared being minimized or cut down? How many of us have said to life, "This is a mistake. I can't do it. It takes more than I've got"?

It does take everything we've got. I walk around the peony bed. Some stems have only one bud. Some have two, and some have as many as six. Soon their peony natures will say "yes" and will open. The petals radiate out—white with pink, pink with white. Can we find it in us to say "yes" like these flowers? And can we support others in their blooming by being a stake, a circle of twine, an encouragement, a loving presence?

*There cannot be a more loving action*
*than being a true support to those persons*
*whom we've been given to know.*

*Sadly, some people feel that they are diminished*
*by giving space, attention, and honor to someone else.*
*These people often have not lived their own blossoming.*
*Another's beauty is then experienced as an internal threat.*

*When we freely act as a stake for another,*
*are we not also supported?*
*The "yes" we offer becomes a "yes" returned.*
*Blossoming is mutual and contagious.*

# *Pond*

A path leads through the underbrush, under the canopy of the ash trees. It's July. The pond is a dark, muddy color. I can see the leaves of many autumns in the bottom of it—russet, brown, and gray. On its surface are water lilies. They float like dreams, lit by a yellow white light. From time to time a bubble rises from the murky bottom as if the roots, too, wanted to touch the surface.

Much is always happening here. The spring peepers are gone now—the heavy plop at the other side of the pond tells me the bullfrogs are out and about. From time to time a frog's call rises like the sound of deep swallowing. And then the chorus starts—like heavy sawing near the waterline.

A young maple leans out over the pond and creates a leafy umbrella. In its shadow, the water's surface reflects more purely. Sky and trees are drawn down here to the level of my feet, yet they are also above me. A dragonfly—electric blue with black wings—lands on a witch hazel leaf next to me. An ancient insect, its color is startling—a shock of iridescent brightness in the foliage.

Below the dreamy, lily-padded water lives a large snapping turtle. I have seen it cruising the bottom. It is awesome to imagine the turtle with its large head, clawed feet, and long tail moving indolently forward. Dragonfly and snapping turtle—the time of ancient creatures is still present in this country garden. I feel stirred when I sense these connections and I feel hopeful, too. Perhaps I haven't been completely tamed yet either.

The pond invites me to imagine and to gaze into it as into an eye, the ground's eye. Minutes expand into hours, into time that is not measured. It feels as if something is gazing back at me, and I am suddenly shy and very small. Exposed, stripped, not of my clothes, but of something else—of a layer that separates me from the world. I shiver and grow quiet.

To gaze into the eye of the ground itself—is it possible? Can the ground be aware of us? This might be too strange to believe. But there is some kind of mutuality. The ground upholds our creatureliness. I believe it knows in its own inimitable way that we breathe and move, that we cry and love, that we are afraid and exultant, that we create and destroy, that we hurt and take care.

There is a feeling of urgency now. I am compelled to notice everything. The wellspring that feeds the pond, and the land that holds this water. I am drawn into the sedge grass, the stones, the moss, and the tree roots that describe the edge of this place. I absorb the brown leaves that make the water dark and reflective. I am imprinted with the maple's shadow, plopped by frogs, sheltered by sky, winged by dragonflies, and moved by a powerful turtle. I am taken to the depth that mirrors my face back to me.

Noon. The heat seems to glaze the surface of the water. In the quiet and dark heart of the pond everything settles down. Deep inside us, can we settle, too, learning to be fluid and yet still?

*When movement and stillness are united,*
*there is a profound peace that,*
*though it travels everywhere, does not disturb anything.*
*Instead it embraces and enhances what it touches.*

*Can a person become like that? Can we let go*
*of self-centeredness and inner clamor enough*
*to become one with what surrounds us?*
*When this happens, we are released from the prison*
*of ego—and for a blessed moment we feel*
*the profound grace of being one with all that is.*

# Daylilies

The daylilies are budding. The flowers will soon come out. There are three varieties here, and they will stagger their blooming from now until the beginning of August. All three are yellow: bright yellow, butter yellow, and salmon yellow. They are a celebration of the sun at its zenith—their brief life is an acknowledgment that each day is a unique blossom.

There is a ring of them near the crescent bed of peonies. There is a bank of them along the stone wall. And since they are profuse and readily multiply, I have moved some to a place near the brook. I could have daylilies everywhere there is sun, just as I have impatiens everywhere there is shade.

Middle of summer is yellow-glory time. When I bring a flower inside and put it in a vase, it illuminates my table, as though the sun were shining inside my house. The lily will stay large and open until midnight. By morning, however, it is limp and wizened, leaving a clear, round drop of moisture on the table. The lily has spent all it had, even its internal moisture. To give one's all—how many of us dare to do that? It is a kind of ecstasy. When we do so for even one small moment, we fulfill something profound inside us.

But we can only give our *all* when we are able to be less self-aware. The need and joy of full expression asks us to stop watching ourselves, evaluating ourselves, or monitoring how others might perceive us. Paradoxically, by letting the ego take a backseat, one's all can step into the light.

I look inside the most yellow of the lilies. It is trumpet-shaped. Looking carefully I see the stamen, the pistil, and I see the mysterious darkness in the neck of the trumpet. Is it from there that all this yellow light pours out?

There is no light without darkness, no joy without sorrow. A great belly laugh can sound like a sob. Life is poignant and deep. We are here to experience it all.

*Sometimes when we encounter great beauty,*
*we shed tears.*
*Sometimes when great happiness fills us,*
*we shed tears.*
*Sometimes when we have spent ourselves completely,*
*we shed tears.*

*Plants and animals might cry just as we humans do—*
*in fact, all that exists may weep and rejoice*
*in some ineffable way that is beyond*
*our usual understanding.*
*Can we sense how all of creation is in deep communion,*
*and that nothing and no one is left out?*

# Hostas

The hostas grow along the stone wall. They have been filling out more and more as the years go by. Big leaves emerge in May and get larger, until by June a deep bank of green lines the wall.

Hostas give shape to the garden. They are large, handsome, and sturdy. Their flowers smell sweet. Later in the summer, you can see the whitish purple bells shine brightly on moonlit nights.

When the flowers have wilted, they produce seeds the birds like. All in all these are steady, no-fuss, no-work plants that make the garden look shapely and complete no matter what else may or may not be blooming.

As a consequence these hostas are easy to take for granted, like anything strong, steady, reliable, constant usually is. There is an "of-course-you'll-continue-to-be-there" attitude one develops with such dependability.

There are people who are like these plants. We do not even know how much we count on them. For us they are background, backbone, and backup. They become somehow invisible to us in their strength and willingness to serve. Then we are totally surprised if anything happens to them.

One summer during a drought, the deer decided to munch up the hostas. Since all the succulent greens had been exhausted in the woods, the deer came to help themselves to this ready produce. I woke up the next morning and found what looked like trimmed celery stalks. No big lush leaves. No dense green border. Only stalks! A scene of devastation.

After that I took more care. I got human hair from the barber to put on the ground, hoping the smell would discourage the deer. I began to appreciate the stately shapes of these hostas. I began to care more for them than for the annuals. I no longer took their steady, sturdy presence for granted.

It is good to become aware of relationships we have taken for granted. Relatives. Old friends. People in the helping professions whom we rely on. They form the background to our foreground. It is important to realize how much we rely on them without thinking, how much shape they give to our lives, how much appreciation they deserve.

*All day and every day there are people and circumstances,*
*known and unknown, that support our lives.*
*How easy it is not to notice this or to simply ignore it.*

*First of all, nature holds us. From the ground up we are*
*supported—earth, air, water, and crops that sustain us.*
*We are because the world is.*

*Around us the existence and work of others*
*make our lives possible.*
*We are because others are.*
*There is nothing that is not somehow mutual*
*and a connection with everything else.*
*What else could we be then but grateful?*

# Black Snake

He lives in the stone wall. A very large snake. In the heat of late July he can sometimes be found basking on the stones. He has a drugged, sleepy quality when I find him in this state because he is letting his cold-blooded nature absorb the high temperatures of these summer days.

The black snake and I are friends. He does not bother me and I do not bother him, but we are aware of each other. He no longer slithers away when I find him. In this mutual living arrangement we acknowledge each other, and we keep the appropriate distance.

Other snakes have always frightened me, but this one does not. He seems like a guardian snake. I know he keeps the mice and chipmunk population down. But he does more. To me he is a representative of an ancient understanding. His very being reminds me that renewal is possible, that skins can and ought to be shed. I once found one of his—transparent and paper-thin like isinglass.

This black snake is elegant, whether coiled or moving. He is like a small, dark river that pours into the stone wall when he wants to, and then is gone. The movement is sensuous. He flows himself forward. His belly feels and knows every inch of the ground. This is intimate indeed.

Sometimes I lie down on the grass to also feel the ground with my belly. Skin on skin: earth skin to human skin. It is good to be held by earth, to shed our old skins and wait for the sun, to be cold when it is cold, to move quickly when it is time to move, and when possible to lie about in happy indolence. This is black snake wisdom. It is no mistake that many indigenous peoples hold animals in reverence. They know of the healing power when we align with particular animals with which we resonate.

The black snake and I—the cold-blooded one and the warm-blooded one—meet at the stone wall, our domains joined for a moment. What do we have in common? The stones and the sun's warmth. The July air and the high cumulus clouds. We have this moment to co-exist and please each other.

To pour ourselves forward when it is time to move and to curl up and relax when it is time to rest seems very good indeed.

*It is no small matter to know and feel that we have*

*the power of our innate life force to renew*

*our ways of being, our perspectives, and our goals.*

*How do we respect that power? How do we use it?*

*These are perennial and challenging questions.*


*The snake has from ancient time been a symbol*

*for the life force and for renewal.*

*Renewal is both longed for and feared.*

*We know that renewed, we will be different.*

*What we once held as true and constant will not be*

*anymore. The unknown opens before us*

*without a designated path.*

*We must make our way by simply going where we sense*

*we need to go.*

# Vines

In the garden, honeysuckle and wild grape grow in profusion. In and of themselves they are wonderful. The night air fills with honeysuckle sweetness, and by day bees and butterflies visit the vines. In August the grapes produce heavy purple clusters for jelly and large, edible leaves for dolmades.

And yet these vines choke trees and bushes. I constantly have to cut the climbers back. There is a persistent clinging going on here, to the point where some trees and bushes perish under the weight. I can feel how silently and steadily the vines take over if I am not on my guard.

When I go to prune them back, I see how skillfully they wrap themselves clockwise around whatever is available. They are the opportunists of the garden, the hangers-on. Tendrils reach out to secure more growing territory. Up the trunk, over the branch, and out into the air, searching for any cling-on place. No respecters of boundaries, they cling wherever they can—relentless, helical, and wondrous. Still, I have to cut them back.

How hard it is for many of us to be similarly persistent when it comes to clinging people. There are always one or two with whom we struggle over boundaries. They are the honeysuckle and the grape in our personal relationships. We want them to be part of our lives, but we do not want them to weigh us down to the ground. To begin with, we might say no, politely. Then we might set up barriers. Even so, the boundary is not always respected.

The nature of honeysuckle and grape is to climb, to grow *upon* something. They cannot be other than how they are. And truthfully, aren't we all somewhat vinelike? We grow upon the strength of others, reaching out for new places of discovery. Our need for support is constant.

The summer nights continue warm and full of stars. I smell the honeysuckle through my window. And in the morning I go hunting for the young grapes. They are filling out, plump and dusty purple.

*Boundaries are places where so much happens.*
*Can we think of boundaries as thresholds?*
*When we cross over a threshold—*
*while honoring the spaces that are marked and*
*delineated—we discover the mutual freedom*
*that respect and courtesy offer.*
*Thresholds can be mindful places of give-and-take.*

*All of us will one day need support.*
*Even so, no matter how insistent our need,*
*it is not a license to mandate another to give us support.*
*Likewise, just because we see a need we are not*
*instantly commanded to provide for it.*
*Circumstances like these need discernment and courtesy.*

*When we pause at the boundary and ask—*
*"May I?" "Can you?" "Is it possible today?"—*
*we live better side by side and are made stronger.*

# Cicadas

The heat has been relentless. Everything seems to pant or wilt or move with appalling effort. At night the cicadas have started their chorus. It is a rather quiet chorus to begin with, but as summer progresses toward autumn the singing seems to intensify and eventually fills the nights to capacity. The dark hours are all sound—waves move into each other and also echo one another. They arise and fall away, only to return again. How many cicadas are out there? Countless, it seems.

I feel a little sad now. Burdened, actually. The heat has something to do with it. I do not want to move my body, and yet I must bear up. It is too hot to work, to play, to plant, or to do anything at all. I feel as if I am both in the sickbed and by the bed of someone sick. It's a heavy feeling.

August is often when wars start, when old folks die, when there are violent storms. Everything seems to have difficulty enduring itself.

Many people go away on vacation in August. I don't feel up to traveling, so I might as well lie in the hammock at night and listen to the cicadas singing out their monotony, their exultation. This is their time—the chanting time.

There are ceremonies where the drum holds a beat for hours, and the same song is sung until one gives into it, until the inner doors swing wide and another dimension opens up. Scientific theories tell us how a critical mass must be reached before a new paradigm can be discovered. It is like birthing. Pain is part of the process. Delivery does not happen without it. This is true in science, in creativity, and in the growth of more consciousness.

Summer draws to a close. The harvest begins. Ripeness can be a burdensome state. The cicadas are wailing. For me this is a time to feel the weight of change. This season I want a friend to be with, someone who will not be shocked if I sometimes want to wail like the cicadas—to release the weight of birthing, the built-up tension that comes with change.

*One bears the pain of change in whatever way one can*
*and as long as one must. Silently it accumulates.*
*If what needs to be birthed has no means of expression,*
*it will come out in an illness, in an accident,*
*or in the rupture of a relationship.*
*Change ripens like a fruit inside us.*
*It must be given its own way to be born.*

*Unlike the cicadas, we might grow silent*
*in the face of change.*
*In the growing awareness of our true tasks, we sense*
*the inherent labor we will have to bear because of them,*
*the pain we will have to endure,*
*the unavoidable exposure these tasks will bring to us.*
*Still, change we must.*

# *Harvest*

Cucumbers, tomatoes, basil, eggplant, peppers, beets, spinach. The crops are coming in now. I might have not done so well with the vegetable garden this year, but well enough to feel rushed, to want to use the produce, to invite people over to help me eat it.

The nasturtiums are in full bloom. Their snappy leaves and flowers fill the salad bowl. The tomatoes are bulging with juice. The pears are yellowing. The plums are collecting on the ground. There is plenty now. When the time for bounty is here we must not dread what might come next. This is the time to open wide, to harvest, to share, and to be as flagrant as nature. It is early September, the time of ripeness.

As I pick cucumbers, I feel their prickly skins on my hand. Eggplants dangle in purple splendor, not as big this year as other years, but glossy and silky of skin. I remember their beginning when they were only mauve four-petaled flowers. My basket is full. Each mature vegetable or fruit has touched me first as seedling or as seed. While they grew, I grew. We have ripened together.

All living things progress from seed to flower to fruit to surrender in some way. But there is also another way, a deepening that points us to what is beyond time—life rejoicing in life, life continuously renewing itself, life living for its own sake without a why.

I gather this harvest to me. I will consume it and make it part of my very flesh even as I harvest experience—

and it, too, becomes part of my very being. I know I live by consuming life. And life is living me, consuming me.

I hold the bounty basket in my arms. On top are the nasturtium flowers. They move in the breeze that has just come over the hill. The red, yellow, orange flowers roll to the basket's rim. Quickly I put a hand over them so they will not fall to the ground. The breeze picks up. The petals shiver. It is all so precious and impermanent. With my hand over this riot of color, I feel this great bounty.

*As we harvest, the air is getting cooler. Very gradually,*
*week by week, the days are growing shorter.*
*Nightfall happens sooner.*
*Fall is coming.*

*In our gardens we begin to clean up the vegetable beds.*
*We prune back what is leggy and has done its work.*
*In the midst of all this bounty is the need to consolidate*
*and simplify. The labor of harvest is clarifying.*
*Fall is coming.*

*Deer move in the woods. Their babies have grown.*
*Birds gather like scudding clouds. They won't leave just yet*
*but they are getting ready to go.*
*Fall is coming.*

*Where will our journey take us now?*
*It deepens with each season, and we can feel*
*more and more what lives with us and in us.*
*Fall is coming.*

# FALL

# Leaves

Leaves. There are so many of them. Piles and piles of them. Each one is singular. Yellow, red, orange, parchment—they sail down in the autumn air like fearless skydivers. They are so trusting, letting go completely. They do not question as I do: Will it be safe? Will I understand? Will it hurt? I am stalling, qualifying, questioning instead of releasing and taking my chances.

In the order of things around my home, the ash trees shed first. Their boat-shaped leaves sail away early and easily. After that the big sugar maple begins. It stands in perfect glory for about a week. Then one night I sense that it sighs deeply somewhere inside its gnarled trunk and says, "Enough." The next day I see a waterfall of leaves. They cascade down, rustling and pouring, to pool upon the ground like a large, golden puddle. Earthlight shimmers up at me.

The pine trees drop many of their needles now, too. But I have also noticed that they shed some needles throughout the seasons. A little at a time, theirs is a whispered letting go. Under each pine the needles form a fragrant carpet of mulch. Weeds seem not to be able to take hold there. If we could constantly shed what is no longer needed, would this help to control the weeds in our lives?

Messy as the leaves are in the garden, their process is direct and clean. When the time comes to let go, they let go. I take up the rake and move the leaves toward the compost pile. They rustle as I rake—a familiar autumn sound.

Letting go is a constant process. Often we cannot know what is happening until months later, sometimes years later. Memory shifts without our knowing about it. The very structure of experience changes. Insights emerge. Our own aging adds its part to this, as does the living of every day. The old breaks down, and we sense something new emerging.

*Letting go, venturing into the unknown,*
*we are not bound by rules and routines.*
*We are not expecting specific outcomes.*
*Instead we are experiencing a lightness of being.*

*Falling leaves are icons of this process.*
*They sail. They glide. They land on the ground.*
*They surrender.*
*They give up their current form.*
*Embraced by the earth, they will in time*
*become holy ground that can support new life.*

# Compost

It's cleanup time in the garden. With the leaves down I weed out the flower beds, getting ready for the first frost. The vegetable garden has been turned over. The impatiens are setting seedpods. In my fist these pods explode like small, green firecrackers. Freed, the little black seeds lie in the crevice of my hand, highlighting the crease the palmists call the lifeline.

Songbirds help themselves to the hosta seeds, and squirrels avidly gather acorns. I pop the last of the late raspberries into my mouth. They are poignantly sweet, a lingering taste of summer. Now puffballs and the ash tree boletus emerge from the ground.

With the wheelbarrow I trudge up to the compost pile, one trip after another. It is growing into a handsome heap. Last year's leaves are now flattened at the bottom of the pile, somewhat decomposed, and underneath it all is a haven for earthworms. They are long and fat at this time of year.

As far as I am concerned, earthworms are the best of gardeners. They are great aerators of soil. By both consuming the compost and moving through it, they open spaces in the packed layers for air to enter. Also, their castings make for wonderful fertilizer. I hope the earthworms will burrow down below the frost line this winter and be able to thrive again come spring. At that time I will hope to put a bunch of them in the vegetable garden.

In my compost pile the leaves are a colorful bunch. There are grass clippings as well as weeds, small twigs, and kitchen leavings. As I turn the pile over, everything joins with everything else. It is hard to know any longer what is what because it is mixed together, on the way to becoming one thing—soil. I take comfort in this. Through the seasons, my hopes, fears, worries, joys, and sorrows are like the compost bits. It all comes together. No experience is ever lost in this universe. Turned over and over, our loves and losses will in time change into something alive and new— the rich, dark earth of experience.

*We might be a little afraid of rot—*
*the stink and mess of it.*
*But if we do not allow a natural death for the things*
*that are over and ready to be composted inside us,*
*we won't create soil for the yet to be.*
*The inner compost process can be perceived*
*as unpleasant and disturbing—*
*or it can simply be allowed.*
*This is mostly a matter of attitude.*

*There are seasons when we are not*
*what we would call "ourselves."*
*They are the fall seasons in our lives.*
*When we shed the past like the trees shed their leaves,*
*the old just drops away. When we embrace this*
*as a natural time of release, we will come to feel*
*the freedom and rightness of it.*

# Feral Cat

I have seen him for several years now. These are only glimpses—maybe two or three in the course of months. I sense him more than I see him—a somewhat savage shadow that moves in the periphery of my vision. His fur is the color of underbrush, thick and matted. He could be mistaken for a raccoon except when he turns his face toward me and looks. Then I can see that he is a feral cat, and very fine. I like knowing that he hunts and survives on this land.

"Him" is how I think of this cat. All my instincts tell me he should have no name, for his power lies in the fact that he is wild and is determined to be so. I wish him whatever comfort he can find.

Once I happened to cross his path in the morning and he hurried under the boxwood with a haughty turn of his head. I felt as if I had stepped on his private domain. And, of course, I had.

My best look at him came one sunny day in mid-November. He had found a bank of leftover leaves where sun would shine for several hours. Snuggled down in brown brush and russet leaves, only his ears were visible. I sensed that he knew I had spotted him.

We sat this way, he in the leaves and I in my chair inside, looking through the window. The sun beat down. The minutes passed and then the hour. I felt akin to him and could feel myself becoming catlike, too. I imagined being out there in the leaves.

I could smell the wet, cold ground somehow, and the slightly dusty odor of leaves. I could feel warmth coming into me, reaching past fur to the bones—white, precise bones. I could hear the rustle of a starling. Not worth hunting. Not worth moving my thawing body for. I could feel the rightness of this warmed bank, this place where no one owed me anything and I was free to be myself, free to care for myself. Hunt when hungry. Rest when tired.

Feeling like "Him" in my imagination, I knew all the places to go on this land. Under the boxwood, into the leaf pile, close to the brush heaps in the woods to wait for grouse or chipmunk. I knew where the water was. I knew where to be when. No special time telling needed. Noon and sun the same thing. Shade and hiding, one. Lunch and rabbit, a perfect unity. Something in me knew when to move and when to be still. My own nature. Taking in the warmth, being here, homelessly at home.

I could see myself through the cat's eyes. I could sense his thinking: "That one behind the glass. She's such a pale thing. No wildness in her. She's limited by safety. Groomed. Careful. Predictable. Let her gaze at me and remember her own fur."

*No fixed address. No given name. Scruffy. Wild.*
*Sensible and living with no trace. We call it feral,*
*but isn't it natural and free? Even if only in the*
*imagination, to have a bit of a feral sensibility*
*might make us live with more confidence.*

*We cannot become something we cannot imagine.*
*We cannot go to what we cannot picture.*
*It is in and through the imagination*
*that we learn to be free.*

*Caution and safety are important. But we also need*
*inner wildness. We need the spaciousness to dream*
*and not be locked into any one pattern or place.*
*That is what it means to be at home in impermanence.*

# Woodpile

Two cords of wood are delivered to my house. The split logs clatter and bounce off the truck bed. Now there is a big pile in the driveway. The wood is for the stove in the living room—seasoned hardwood that will burn slowly and well.

The job of stacking the wood awaits me. This is work that will take most of the day and will make me tired. I know I could be more efficient using a wheelbarrow, but I like carrying the fragrant wood in my arms. I can handle four split logs at a time.

The wood must be placed off the ground and not too close to the house so that boring insects are kept away. I want the woodpile near the house, however, so that if the wind is howling and the snow is whirling I don't have too far to go to fetch what I need.

Slowly the wood stacks up. I love the measure of a cord. I love the beauty of the logs nestling against each other, and I like tucking them under the blue tarp so they will stay dry. I have grown very warm doing this work, and these logs will in turn keep me warm when winter really sets in.

There is a rhythm to carrying this wood armful by armful. All rhythmic work has a kind of grace to it. We can feel quietness inside such work, a sense of peace. Rhythmic work is helped by song. I find myself humming as the task gets done.

Eventually I have to stop as dusk comes earlier now.

It has been a good day. I am glad that I can prepare for winter. There are countless people without shelter and they are not absent from my mind. I almost feel ashamed that I can have this future warmth. A year or two ago, these logs were trees carrying a rich canopy of green leaves. Then they were felled, split, and laid out to dry. I do not take this for granted. They will help me survive the winter. How stark is the truth that sacrifice is at the heart of life.

*Any time we labor at something prolonged*
*we have a chance of finding a working rhythm—*
*be it stacking wood, folding clothes, mowing the lawn,*
*weeding, or chopping vegetables.*
*In rhythm our bodies move with the task more naturally,*
*and chores become not only pleasurable*
*but are also done more easily.*

*With awareness we can intuit rhythms in all we do.*
*Our days have inherent patterns to them*
*if we pay close attention—waking and sleeping,*
*working and playing, focusing and drifting,*
*giving and taking, sacrificing and receiving.*

*Our hearts beat in rhythm,*
*our lungs fill and empty in rhythm.*
*Consciously embracing the natural patterns of our bodies,*
*our days, our work, and the seasons of the year*
*reveals that everything has a rhythm of sorts.*
*Deep in this pattern is a grace that can lead us*
*into wordless peace.*

# Mice

It's almost Thanksgiving, and the herb and vegetable gardens are fully cleaned up. Dry stalks of tomato plants and twiggy stems of rosemary have been pulled from the ground. The yellow snarl of frozen nasturtium and the upright black-spotted remains of basil have been removed. Now I can see various holes dug by little creatures in the ground. Food supplies are tucked away by them, and strategic entries made into the cellar of the farmhouse. I know, because I hear cautious scurrying at night. The field mice are taking up their winter residence.

There is no way to keep them out of my house. The foundation is stone without mortar. I have to share the place. The truth is that we live side by side. There is only one of me, and quite a few of them.

One year all my grass seed was consumed. I had carefully put it away in a plastic bag in the garage, but by spring it was nothing but chaff. At first I felt upset. Was my place infested? Were the mice chewing the electrical wires? Would I have to keep everything in metal tins? I put out traps. But weeks later there were still mice in the cellar, and I did not want to use poison. But I also did not want to let the situation get out of hand.

I could not solve this quandary. Instead, my attitude changed. It happened one day that spring when I inadvertently found a mouse nest on a shelf in the garage, built into a cotton drop cloth. Curled up in the nest were six baby mice—blind, hairless, and oh so vulnerable. I could see their hearts beating right through their transparent skins. Their little chests heaved with each breath. They were a pink pulsing so sheer it could be snuffed out in an instant. To be born is to be utterly exposed. It is pure newness.

Each time we come into newness we, too, are pink like this, pulsing and vulnerable. New relationships, new dwellings, new jobs, new understandings. When such change happens, our eyes are so new they aren't able to focus yet. Our skin is paper-thin. It is always a sheer time, an intimate time, when—like all newborns—we need protection badly.

So of course I left the nest just where it was, and some of my intolerant attitude with it. Two weeks later the baby mice were gone. They were in the field, being field mice, not house mice. I shook out the drop cloth and thought about the "able" in the word "vulnerable." *Able* to sustain injury.

Mice, who seem so skittish and afraid, are actually a brave lot. Their tiny black button eyes are unquestioning and steady. They show us a new definition of brave—to feel the fear one has and to own it. Those who deny their fear are not brave.

The mice come and go. They know the ins and outs of the place. When I am having Thanksgiving turkey, they are having grass seeds. So far they have not taken over the house. The feral cat and the black snake keep the mouse population under control. Now when I hear rustling under the sink I am more willing to share. This has been their home territory for generations.

*Sometimes we have to live with something unpleasant,*
*something we deal with as best we can, but something*
*that will ultimately not go away.*
*We may try to take steps to rectify the situation,*
*but the biggest step is an internal one—*
*the step of letting be what is.*

*This can feel like defeat or an opportunity to complain*
*and blame. But it is really an acknowledgment*
*that we have no power to alter the situation.*

*This kind of acceptance changes everything.*
*It is not about giving approval. Nor is it about submission.*
*It is not about mere tolerance, either.*
*It has to do with kindness.*
*With kindness, many things can be endured.*
*With kindness, things mysteriously change*
*on their own accord—and often for the better.*

# Thanksgiving

The skies have been gray for days on end. The woodstove is already warming the living room. I feel snug and ready for winter. Still the out-of-doors calls me. I want to "walk the line," which means walking the property line to check that all things are in order.

Scarf around my neck and wearing a warm jacket, I set off and find that I want to walk farther than "the line." There is a parcel of land near my farmhouse that is just forest. It has some trails in it, but mostly it is unused and wild.

There is no sign prohibiting entry, and so I decide to take a little deer trail among the trees. Away from the road, silence suddenly envelops me. I breathe it in and sense how much I have needed stillness after all the work of the fall season.

Bare trunks rise around me. I stand still like one of the alders and feel rooted in place. How quiet quietness can be. How utterly delicious. For me to have this time of nothingness is everything. I sense the deeper truth of not doing and just being. I wonder if thanksgiving is a natural response for all of us when we are restored back to being.

I feel the woods breathing with me. I need not go anywhere or do anything.

I stand here quietly for a long time, when out of the underbrush a flock of wild turkeys comes slowly toward me. They have not noticed me, or if they have, my stillness has allowed them to feel safe. As they waddle forward I can hear their intimate turkey talk. They are clearly communicating while foraging along the ground, having a Thanksgiving feast.

Eventually I have to move. At once the male picks up his handsome head and seems to give a command. The birds line up single file and march off as fast as they can, in a kind of Thanksgiving parade all their own. Soon they have disappeared, and it's time for me, too, to head home.

*The silence and depth of the forest make us realize*
*there is no "owning" the place where we live.*
*We pay the property taxes, but we possess nothing*
*permanently.*
*Any property line is arbitrary, just a record in a book*
*stored in a town hall.*
*All that grows and lives in these woods belongs here.*

*In moments of utter quiet—*
*when so much that is extraneous falls away—*
*we can see the world in its beauty.*
*Everything has a place and belongs to no one.*
*We own nothing and are owed nothing.*
*Even our bodies are on loan.*
*We have been gifted and trusted with life.*
*That is the Thanksgiving feast.*

# WINTER

# *Bulldog*

Strictly speaking, my neighbor's dog does not reside in my garden. He lives down the road. Still and all, I feel he lives here, too, for he is in my yard often enough. His body, only a few inches off the ground, wags its way into the driveway. His coat is an auburn, almost red color and ripples around him. He is a very fat English bulldog of some advanced years.

His face looks as if he had pressed it up against the shop window of a dog delicatessen for weeks on end. I think his customary drool comes from gazing at those juicy bones displayed behind that window. He lifts his face toward me with the innocence of a child and waits for me to love him.

Of course, I stop everything and give him the attention his unself-conscious and enthusiastic presence seems to require. There is something natural, nonchalant, and humorous about his behavior. I smile and pet him, and feel something else as well, something uncomfortable. When I look deeper into this discomfort, I know I am embarrassed by him.

His delight is obvious and flagrant. He turns over and presents his roly-poly stomach for stroking. "Put your hand right there. Good! And now a little higher, please." Wiggle, wiggle, the sausage body moves along the loose stones of the driveway. He positions himself to get the perfect sensations. There seems to be no pride in the dog, just direct, unadulterated pleasure seeking.

How different life would be for us if we could be as

lacking in self-doubt and self-judgment as this dog. His whole being demonstrates an assumption that he is a lovable creature, a deserving creature, and an enjoyable one. His fat, aged self simply squirms with the sacred knowledge that he is one of God's creatures.

To act as if one had the total endorsement of the universe behind one's particular existence would be extraordinary! We often hedge our bets by offering what we ourselves want, and by restricting our requests for love and help to those we know will not reject us out of hand. We are so careful, whereas we could, with a doglike trust, meet the world with a joyful, natural wag.

I observe the dog's ease and lack of inhibition. I want to learn from him. He lies in the middle of the driveway where the sun shines and warms the stones. If he must, he moves for visitors and their cars. If it should happen that his desirous, loving nature is not met with enough affection, he walks off with a "too-bad-for-her" attitude and seeks his own counsel in a sunny patch under the mailbox. But not for long will this dear dog reject because he was rejected. He will be open to pleasure again—meeting me and anyone else with renewed interest in the possibilities of exchange. No smoldering grudges or careful tallies of past slights here.

This dog is not, in fact, trying to attain something. He is simply meeting the world with his pleasure-nature, inviting those who can join his radiance—light with light. I want to participate in this direct and happy warmth. I want to let my love and pleasure out so it can meet the love and pleasure of others directly.

*Such animal and person exchanges can thaw us—*
*a little at a time.*
*To keep our inner sunlight locked away is painful and*
*wintry. We hide it to feel safe, and because*
*we have been conditioned to do so.*
*What if we could be conditioned to be radiant*
*instead of protective?*

*When we smile, for instance, all sorts of benign chemistry*
*happens in our bodies.*
*In exchanging smiles with a baby or a stranger,*
*we make the world warmer for them and for ourselves.*
*The gift of such simple friendliness has unaccountable*
*benefits.*

*The love at the heart of the universe is there for you*
*and me and for all creatures.*
*It is the true bond we share.*
*Allowing more and more of it in,*
*we can let more and more of it out.*

# Ash Trees

It is late December. The trees stand naked. Stripped, they have a sculptured look, and I have the curious sensation that I can both see and hear better in these winter woods. The wind is blowing hard. Above my head, tree limbs are clashing, making boisterous, wooden music. Here below, where I stand, the trunks seem to glow. On their bark, the lichen shimmers in the blue-gray light of this season. Subtle, muted colors—ochre, gray-white, and the palest moss green. They are the patinas made by slow, quiet growth.

This is the stuff of life and of art. Nothing dramatic. Just years of persistence. Growing in the same place. Extending a little farther. Becoming a little more. A quiet work that enlarges by seasons.

What is homely and seemingly inconsequential becomes important in winter. In this woodlot of ash trees and brush, one little bush shines with red berries. The berries seem to shout with color. "We are here," they call to the birds. "Eat us, digest us, drop us, and spread our seeds so we can multiply." This is interrelatedness with a purpose.

But the berries do something else as well with no obvious purpose. Their color, in this otherwise brown and gray canvas, makes it possible to see everything more clearly. Twenty red berries in an acre of brown. The trees make the berries more visible. The berries make the trees more visible. They reveal and reflect one another and yet remain independent. Together they are more without losing themselves. In the winter light this is so visible to me. It is pure interplay. I want my human relationships to have this intimacy and ease.

Bare bones of ash trees. Shimmering berries. Lichen growing without ambition, just true to its lichen nature. When we allow ourselves to be and allow others to be just as they are, what wonderful bare bones of connection we have. When we can notice and savor the many flashes of color that happen in life, the bright berries of delight, what constant praise that is. When we can be patient and know that what develops consistently over time, little by little, is what ultimately is rewarded and lasts, what wonderful relaxation in growth that is. We can stop hurrying to be what we cannot yet be, and rest simply in what we are now.

Above me, the leafless crowns of the ash trees move against each other. The sound is that of wooden tongues speaking or singing a foreign language with glottal stops. I do not understand a word, but I feel the music. Something happens in my belly when I hear it. Somehow I am singing, too, and being sung. It is a different kind of understanding. High above my head a grand, important orchestra is playing the winter chorale of the ash trees.

Wooden voices sing a cappella in the chill wind. I listen and feel the wordless branches in myself joining the allegro. The winter solstice has passed. The dark turns again to light. I sing the turning of the year. I sing the season. I sing with whatever can sing. Let all that has life be glad. Clap hands and branches. More understanding than any life can wish for is this urge to praise. Rejoice and again rejoice.

*Joy is a sign of the spirit. It is different from happiness.*
*Joy simply "is." Happiness, on the other hand,*
*is always tied to something temporal and impermanent.*
*Joy is timeless and inclusive. It cannot be joy*
*without including what is not yet in joy.*
*It waits for us to open our hearts,*
*to let the hymn of the universe sing.*
*If we are not yet able to sing, joy will not despise us.*
*It accepts even a humble humming.*

# Storm

The lowering sky and the weather report both confirm a major storm from the west hurtling in our direction. There are longer lines at the grocery store. People are stocking up for the siege. The snow shovel is inside the house. Now things will happen as they will.

The first flakes dance past the windows. In an hour, the garden has a dusting like confectioners' sugar on a cake. Two hours later there are no dark patches anywhere. Dusk is falling. The wind howls. Already the lights have flickered on and off. At nine in the evening the power goes off. I light my candle and feel how the house rocks a little when the wind surges. In a strange way it feels like a ship creaking and rolling at sea. This is a serious storm.

I debate whether to light a fire and keep the living room warm through the night, but I am tired, too tired to stay up and tend it. There is no good place to be except in bed, but first I open every faucet in the house just a little so the water can drip to prevent the pipes from freezing. With a sweater over my pajamas and two extra blankets, I curl up like the animal I am, like all the animals beyond these doors that must survive this storm.

All through the night the wind howls. It sounds like a beast that wants to come in from the cold. Slowly I feel a prayer of solidarity cover me like skin. This is a prayer for all those who have no shelter this night. May they be taken in and be cared for. Any one of us, for no reason at all, could find ourselves in such straits. Serious storms come to all of us in life and in many forms—accidents, unemployment, illness, political upheaval, and loss of loved ones. Such storms do not go away like this wintry one will in twenty-four hours. Without help it is hard to survive them.

Daybreak. My house feels like an old-fashioned icebox. As I try to light the fire, my hands shake. Finally, a curl of smoke finds its way up the chimney. The draft will do the rest. Soon there will be flames. I go to the back door and see the snow packed three feet high against it. From every window I see nothing but white, white, and more white. For now I am a creature alone in her den. I will not force a way out.

Snow continues to fall, but the center of the storm has moved on. A lovely silence has come. This quiet opens a door to a time within time. I want to take it into every cell of my body, into my being and my longing heart.

*The ancient contemplatives of the desert said that we need*
*to learn everything within the confines of our cells*
*or simple dwellings, and that we must stay in them*
*and near them to take the journey to the heart*
*where God dwells and is the deepest truth.*

*By not looking outward for sustenance or diversion,*
*we encounter who we really are—*
*vulnerable in our patterns of avoidance,*
*vulnerable in our fears and our longings,*
*vulnerable in our human wounds.*
*It is in our vulnerable humanity, not in our strength*
*and confidence, that Spirit finds us and claims us.*

# Tracks

Early January. The new calendar year has started. New snow has fallen. It's like a sheet of beautiful white paper—a parchment ready for tracks to be laid down on it. One can study life-as-lived in animal tracks, life-as-process, the marks of what has been and still is.

We can dream ourselves into those blue-black shadows in the snow and sense the motivation of another creature. In the white snow cover of our minds, our intentions are making tracks all the time. There are beaten paths, entrenched habits, that keep us from exploring new ground. But we are often not aware of those trails and how deeply they have been laid down in us. We do not even know the self who treads upon them.

To study motivation is to study one's own tracks. Is there time to catch that movement which is before movement? The movement, like an animal's instinct, prior to thought, and alive in the very cells of the body. The movement, which forms thought and is the substance and event of thought. This is where those old predators, fear and desire, can be faced. This is the place where true self-knowing will be discovered, if it ever can be.

In the fine white snow of this January day, I see how a rabbit came this way past the brushy piles by the stone wall. Was it escaping, running in fear? Was it foraging, trying to feed the gnawing in its stomach? Was it leaping for the sheer joy of movement? Rabbit tracks. I dream myself into the creature that made them. So much like me—heart pounding a mile a minute, often stopped and frozen in fear, or scurrying for cover.

I follow the rabbit's path. The back paws leave bigger shadows. There is something steady in the space between the front paws and the back ones, and in the repeating of their pattern. One time last winter I saw some strange rabbit tracks: hop, hop, hop—and then they completely stopped. No broken snow. No evidence of violence. No explanation. No continuation. Nothing but white, untouched snow.

Was the rabbit transmuted? Did it simply ascend? It was a mystery. How life-giving the unsolvable is. I want to live with Mystery—bounding into the heart of the world, into the new snow of this moment and the new year.

*To embrace Mystery is to live without prior assumptions.*
*It is to live with questions instead of ready answers.*
*Maybe it is about learning to live with the discomfort*
*and excitement of uncertainty.*
*Maybe it is to be in constant discovery,*
*even if what we discover is something we've known before.*
*It will be new nonetheless.*

*To live with Mystery is to be open to wonder—*
*to questioning and to awe. It means to live*
*without self-preservation as our first priority.*
*We lay down our tracks every day as if in new snow.*
*We make a path that was not there before.*

# Thaw

February. The days are getting lighter. I feel relief. The sun, for the past two weeks or more, is warmer. I can hear the water running in the brook, which was dry only a few weeks back. Everything is trickling. Little rivulets of water move in the grass, among tree roots, under the leaves. Walking out in the woods I find that my boots stick in the soft ground.

I am celebrating this wet earth. I am celebrating a break in the below-twenty-degree weather that has been relentless for the past weeks. February thaw—messy and wonderful. I can almost sniff spring, but I also know that the ground will freeze again, and that more cold is yet to come.

This is the time to see what winter damage has happened in the garden. It is the time to pore over seed catalogs—and to keep my gardener's greed in check. Living alone, I know I am limited in what I can do in the garden. I have to be willing to look at the glossy catalogs and say, "NO."

In this mild winter weather, everything appears hopeful and possible. A little more sun and the garden looks as if it is already blooming—weed-free and glorious. But this is an image I have learned not to trust, for by late June, with too much to take care of, the pleasure of gardening can turn into a chore, robbing me of leisure and hence of delight.

Leisure and delight—they are wedded. Without leisure, there is no time to feel and to savor. In leisure and delight there is a rhythm that allows things to grow at an organic pace. When I really match that pace, I sense that the "inmost" garden of the world is fundamentally one of leisure. Vegetation has its seasons. The moon has its month. The sun has its day. The universe is orderly and is always on time.

I look at the seed catalogs, and from them I get an artificial sense that at any time of the year, anything can be made to be grown. With effort and at a price! If I forced flowers, started seeds indoors, bought artificial light, I could have something splendid even now in late winter. But this, I have learned, is not for me. Having lost my leisure over and over again, I must be abstinent now in order to have what I really need—time to feel and to be in the place I live. It's February and that means it is winter still, a time when I can be spare and love it.

Out into this mild, winter weather I go to reconnoiter and to pick up small sticks for kindling. I cannot do anything about the garden now. This is the season when the garden is truly and simply lying fallow. And I must follow suit. In that state, restoration goes on in ways that are not apparent and are yet essential. For me, that means going out into the world of snow puddles and melting icicles instead of ordering seeds. It means experiencing the land without a plan for it.

I listen to the brook. It moves along at a happy, burbling pace, flowing with a steady volume. It stays within its banks. It follows the path of least resistance and is yet consistent with itself. Trickling, gurgling, bubbling. On it goes. Not missing any ground it travels over. Filling up the hollow spaces. Moving on. Moving on. I want to live this way. Staying within my capacity. Filling the space. Enjoying each season. Planting, cultivating, pruning, harvesting, lying fallow. Moving on in God's time, leisure time. Thawing time.

Spare. Knowing that less is more. Less need to improve,
less trying, less judgment, less regret.
We need to learn this, year after year.
Slowly the self-imposed abstinence gives us freedom.
But this is not always an easy process.

To do little, but with great consciousness and respect,
is to do more than we might realize.
Our goals do not consume our personhoods.
And we do not then consume each other,
and use less of the earth's resources.

To say "no" to hurry, to overwork,
to whatever is more than is needed,
is to say "yes" to leisure, to reverie, and communion.

# Geese

Geese are flying over. Sometimes there are only a few of them. Sometimes there are twenty or more geese flying in formation. I get a rush of hopeful feeling when I hear them honking. I have never completely understood why. At first I thought it was because they had the freedom of the skyways—something high and romantic—something in contrast to my earthbound existence. But since then I have learned more about geese. This new information has fleshed out that spontaneous inner feeling of mine.

Geese depend on one another. The lead goose does the most work, but when it is tired, it falls back and another takes its place. The leadership is shared. Being in charge for them is not about ego or control, but about what will serve the flock in the best way.

All of us have gifts that can benefit others. How different our world would be if we all acted with the community in mind. Our strengths could be expressed for the benefit of the whole, and we could sense how necessary mutuality is in the handling of our challenges.

To be able to rely on others is a deep trust that does not come easily. But if we let go of needing to be special or superior, our journeys can become easier. The geese fly in the wake of one another's wings. They literally get a lift from each other. Can we be with others this way? Geese show us that it is possible to fly long and far when we have support.

The high honking I hear when I stand on the ground

and look up is the sound of encouragement the geese make to keep on flying. It is a loud and happy sound. They are signaling that the journey is as much about communion and community as it is about their destination.

Our journeys are earthbound, but we know that the soul has a propensity to fly. That yearning is always trying to lift us. We are rooted in the finite world, but we know that we belong to something ineffable and much larger.

*Our mandate in life is to become all that we can be.*
*That becoming is ultimately not for ourselves*
*but for the common good and for life itself.*

*We need to remember that whatever our achievements are,*
*they are not personal in the end but interpersonal.*
*In such a way we are all brought to what feels*
*like living water—where we can rest, feed, and be together.*
*It is through such communion that our journeys take us*
*into a common and shared joy.*

# SPRING
# AGAIN

# Wildflowers

The leaves are out. They are a sheer light green, and I am surprised by their shadows. This shade has been absent for months. Now I see patterns on the ground again, patches of dark and light. My feet walk a dappled path.

A sweet smell wafts toward the house from the woods. Years ago when I first smelled it, I thought one special plant must be the source. It took a while to determine that this scent was the essence of these woods, a combination of organic matter, young ferns, and wildflowers. Now every spring I am waiting for that odor. It is a smell that is utterly intimate. It opens me.

These are the days to hunt for Dutchman's-breeches, patches of green with a hovering cloud of white pantaloon-like flowers. Now is the time to find the light pink of wild geraniums and the deep magenta of trilliums. Solomon's seal is out. The ferns are uncurling. Jack is preaching in his pulpit. Indian pipe and lady's slipper are also emerging. They are all here in their appointed places. I love finding them again and again, predictable and wild, elusive and perennial. The woods fill with their sweetness.

In spiritual texts there is mention of perfumed states of being. In deep concentration, odors can arise so honey-like that one is called to remember the beauty of the soul. Maybe that is why we are drawn to very specific fragrances. They remind us of our deepest being. And is not smell the most intimate of the senses? We breathe it deeply into us. We inhale a soul scent and take it to heart.

The wildflowers help me to remember the steadiness of return, year after year. They tell me that one does not need to be cultivated to be beautiful. They tell me that the soul remembers its essence when it is given room to grow. I treasure the shy trillium, the wild geranium, the jack-in-the-pulpit, the lady's slipper, the Dutchman's-breeches, the Indian pipes, Solomon's seal, and the ferns.

These wildflowers are reminders that our life journey has many seasons. On one level it is a visible journey. We live in certain places. We have specific interests and particular work. We love the precious human persons who are our parents, our partners, our children, our friends. These are the components of our visible life.

But there is another journey happening at the same time. It is not so visible.

Our soul journey moves in the cycles and the landscapes of our inner world. It is a journey that gives meaning to our visible lives and leads us to the center—not a destination but a state of being. It is toward that center that we journey.

The scent of the wildflowers reminds us that the journey is ultimately one of surrender. We surrender to no one in the end but to our own soul, to the delicacy and essence of ourselves, which is hidden in God. Sweet and wild is the experience of surrender. There is nothing more intimate.

The seasons of a year. The return of spring.
The heart grows glad when it can leaf out,
when light and shadow are known to belong to
one another.

Our inner journeys have dark, wintry times
and shining seasons with color and abundance.
This is the natural state of things
that does not need to be resisted.
It is organic and builds a capacity to trust, a capacity
that allows us to embrace all the seasons of our lives,
whether they be dark or light.

Through the years we are given to live,
our souls are always longing to grow and mature.
Over time we find that the journey takes us closer and
closer to the place that has always held us
and yearns for us to be greening,
to leaf out, to be fully and fragrantly verdant.

# THE PATH

*How did this journey begin—*
*a path opening from there to here?*
*Perhaps it was in a thicket of trees, thorns,*
*and the soft footfalls of a deer picking her way*
*to berries and water—both of us shy, but*
*not in a hurry. Mimicking the shadows around us*
*we melt, grazing in and out of light.*

*I hear other deer follow, leisurely chewing*
*young leaves. Their munching is gentle and slow.*
*By coming here often our foot prints deepen a path.*
*Above us breezes scuttle in the canopy of alders.*
*How many times have I walked here*
*to be made all over again, to see the moss grow*
*over boulders, steadily greening even on stone?*